Cambridge English

Starters

AUTHENTIC EXAMINATION PAPERS

1

T0349621

STUDENT'S BOOK

Cambridge University Press
www.cambridge.org/elt

Cambridge Assessment English
www.cambridgeenglish.org

Information on this title: www.cambridge.org/9781316635896

© Cambridge University Press and UCLES 2017

First published 2017

30 29 28 27 26 25 24 23 22 21

Printed in Malaysia by Vivar Printing

A catalogue record for this publication is available from the British Library

ISBN 978-1-316-63589-6 Student's Book
ISBN 978-1-316-63593-3 Answer Booklet
ISBN 978-1-316-63597-1 Audio CD

Contents

Listening

Part 1
– 5 questions –

Listen and draw lines. There is one example.

Mark   Eva   Dan   Alice

Grace   Nick   Alex

Part 2

– 5 questions –

**Read the question. Listen and write a name or a number.
There are two examples.**

Examples

What is the boy's name? .... Tom ....

How old is he? .... 11 ....

Questions

1   What is Tom's friend's name?   ....

2   How old is Tom's friend?   ....

3   How many brothers has Tom's friend got?   ....

4   How many children are in Tom's class?   ....

5   What is the name of Tom's teacher?   Mrs ....

Part 3

– 5 questions –

Listen and tick (✔) the box. There is one example.

Which is Kim's bag?

A ✔   B ☐   C ☐

1   What is Anna taking to school?

A ☐   B ☐   C ☐

2   Which is Bill's dad?

A ☐   B ☐   C ☐

3 What would Sam like to do?

A ☐ B ☐ C ☐

4 Which is Jill's bedroom?

A ☐ B ☐ C ☐

5 Which is Nick's brother?

A ☐ B ☐ C ☐

Part 4

– 5 questions –

Listen and colour. There is one example.

Reading and Writing

Part 1
– 5 questions –

Look and read. Put a tick (✔) or a cross (✗) in the box.
There are two examples.

Examples

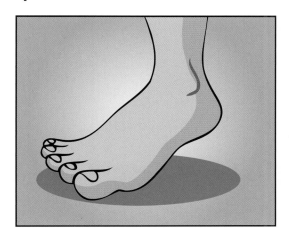

This is a foot.

These are pianos.

Questions

1

This is a train.

2

These are sausages.

3

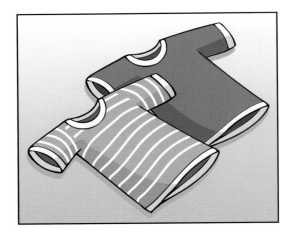

These are skirts.

4

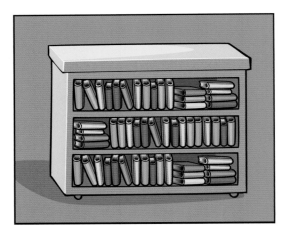

This is a lamp.

5

This is a watch.

Part 2
– 5 questions –

Look and read. Write yes or no.

Examples

A young child is waving. ....*yes*...................

The woman's bag is in her hand. ....*no*...................

Questions

1   Two people are wearing red shorts. ....

2   The door of the house is closed. ....

3   The dog has brown ears. ....

4   The girl in a blue jacket is talking. ....

5   The man with black hair is driving. ....

Part 3
– 5 questions –

Look at the pictures. Look at the letters. Write the words.

Example

<u>l i m e</u>

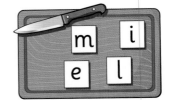

Questions

1

_ _ _ _

2

_ _ _ _ _

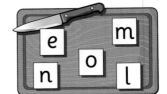

3

_ _ _ _ _ _

4

_ _ _ _ _ _

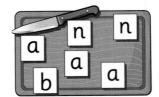

5

_ _ _ _ _ _ _ _ _

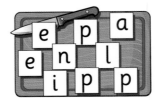

Part 4

– 5 questions –

Read this. Choose a word from the box. Write the correct word next to numbers 1–5. There is one example.

A chair

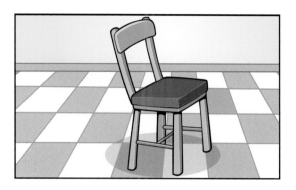

Chairs have four ...*legs*.... . In Mark's flat there are chairs next to the

table in the **(1)** .... Mark's family sit and eat their

(2) .... there. There's a chair in Mark's bedroom too.

Mark sits on his chair and reads his **(3)** .... , listens

to his radio or plays on his **(4)** .... There's a big red

and blue **(5)** .... on the floor under his chair.

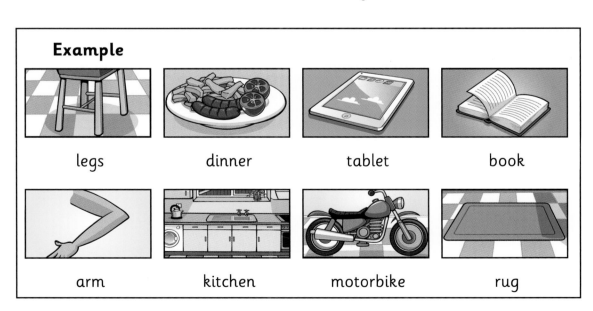

Example

| legs | dinner | tablet | book |
| arm | kitchen | motorbike | rug |

Part 5
– 5 questions –

Look at the pictures and read the questions. Write one-word answers.

Examples

Which animal is drinking?   the .... hippo ....

What are the children doing?   .... painting ....

Questions

1 Who is wearing a hat?   the ....

2   How many animals are drinking now?   ....

3   What is jumping from the tree?   a ....

4   Which child is not happy?   the ....

5   What is the boy doing?   smiling and ....

Blank Page

Part 1
– 5 questions –

Listen and draw lines. There is one example.

Mark   Jill   Pat   Alice

Tom   Grace   Hugo

Part 2

– 5 questions –

Read the question. Listen and write a name or a number.
There are two examples.

Examples

What is the name of May's toy monster? .... Pink

How old is the monster? ....2...............................

Questions

1   What number is Pink's bus?   ....

2   What is the name of Pink's school?   .... School

3   How many legs has Pink got?   ....

4   What is the name of the chicken?   ....

5   How many eggs has the chicken got?   ....

Part 3

– 5 questions –

Listen and tick (✔) the box. There is one example.

What is Bill wearing?

A ✔   B ☐   C ☐

1   What is Pat's favourite animal?

  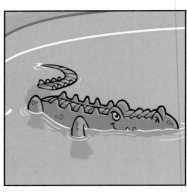

A ☐   B ☐   C ☐

2   What is Anna's grandmother doing?

A ☐   B ☐   C ☐

3   What can the baby do?

A ☐   B ☐   C ☐

4   What does Sam want?

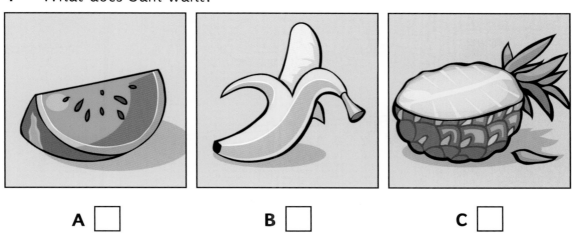

A ☐   B ☐   C ☐

5   Where is the computer?

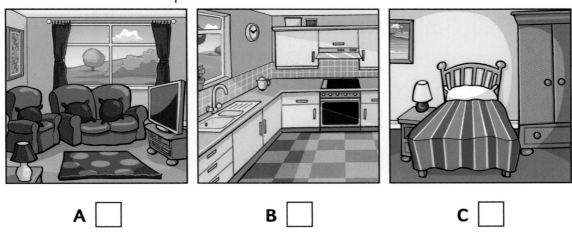

A ☐   B ☐   C ☐

Part 4

– 5 questions –

Listen and colour. There is one example.

Reading and Writing

Part 1
– 5 questions –

**Look and read. Put a tick (✔) or a cross (✗) in the box.
There are two examples.**

Examples

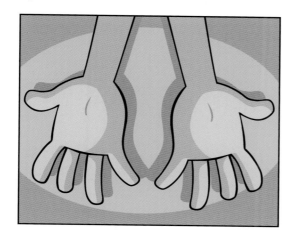

These are hands.

This is a radio.

Questions

1

This is a handbag.

2

This is a lamp. ☐

3

These are polar bears. ☐

4

This is a robot. ☐

5

This is a motorbike. ☐

Part 2
– 5 questions –

Look and read. Write yes or no.

Examples

There is a mirror on the wall.	............................yes............................
The baby is having a bath.	............................no............................

Questions

1 Some clothes are on the chair. ....

2 The boy has got brown hair. ....

3 There are three boats in the water. ....

4 There is a rug on the floor. ....

5 The girl is wearing green socks. ....

Part 3
– 5 questions –

Look at the pictures. Look at the letters. Write the words.

Example

<u>p e a r</u>

Questions

1

_ _ _ _

2

_ _ _ _ _

3

_ _ _ _ _

4

_ _ _ _ _ _

5

_ _ _ _ _ _

Part 4
– 5 questions –

Read this. Choose a word from the box. Write the correct word next to numbers 1–5. There is one example.

A living room

You find a living room in a ...house... or flat. Ben's living room has

a door and two windows. His living room is between the dining

room and the **(1)** .... Ben's family watches

(2) .... in the living room. Ben and his sister sit

on the **(3)** .... and play games there. Ben's mum

plays a **(4)** .... in the living room. There are

(5) .... of the family on the wall.

Example			
house	piano	kiwi	kitchen
television	ruler	pictures	sofa

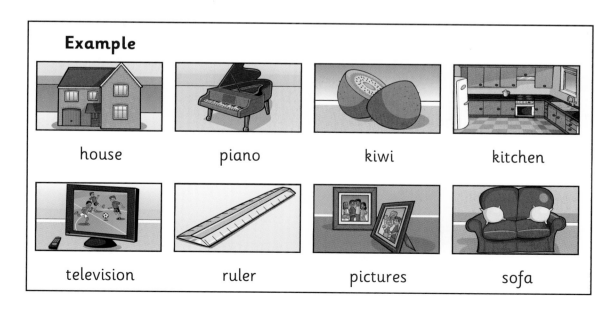

Part 5
– 5 questions –

Look at the pictures and read the questions. Write one-word answers.

Examples

Where are the children and
their father?

in the .... *garden* ....

What are the two brothers playing?

.... *football* ....

Questions

1   Where is the ball?

on the ....

2   What is the ball hitting now?   ....

3   What is the bird doing?   ....

4   Where is the cat?   in the ....

5   What are the boys playing with now?   a ....

Blank Page

Listening

Part 1
– 5 questions –

Listen and draw lines. There is one example.

Matt   Tom   Hugo   Lucy

Sue   Jill   Alex

Part 2
– 5 questions –

**Read the question. Listen and write a name or a number.
There are two examples.**

Examples

What is the boy's name? .... Bill ....

How many arms has the monster got? .... 6 ....

Reading and Writing

Part 1
– 5 questions –

Look and read. Put a tick (✔) or a cross (✗) in the box.
There are two examples.

Examples

These are shoes.

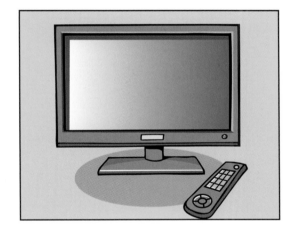

This is a keyboard.

Questions

1

This is a kite.

2

These are crayons. ☐

3

This is a lemon. ☐

4

This is a spider. ☐

5

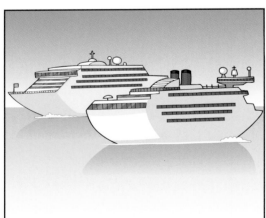

These are ships. ☐

Part 2

– 5 questions –

Look and read. Write yes or no.

Examples

The boy and girl are waving.	*yes*
Some birds are sitting in a tree.	*no*

Questions

1 The man with black hair is taking a photo. ....

2 The door of the house is open. ....

3 A baby is playing with his toys. ....

4 The woman in the garden is wearing a red dress. ....

5 The brown horse has a white tail. ....

Part 3

– 5 questions –

Look at the pictures. Look at the letters. Write the words.

Example

<u>b</u> <u>a</u> <u>t</u> <u>h</u>

Questions

1

— — — —

2

— — — —

3

— — — — —

4

— — — — — —

5

— — — — — — — —

Part 4

– 5 questions –

Read this. Choose a word from the box. Write the correct word next to numbers 1–5. There is one example.

A beach

Beaches are next to the ......sea...... . People like going to the beach. They

wear **(1)** .... on their heads. Some people go to sleep

and some sit and read **(2)** .... there.

Children run on the **(3)** .... or play

(4) .... with their friends. **(5)** ....

live in the water and children like catching them. You can find beautiful

shells on beaches too.

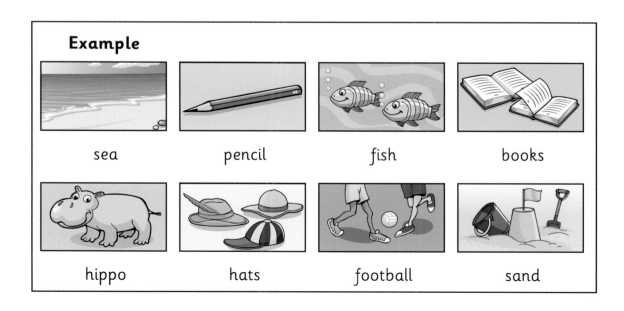

Part 5
– 5 questions –

Look at the pictures and read the questions. Write one-word answers.

Examples

What is the boy bouncing?   a .... *ball* ....

How many people are sitting at the table?   .... *two* ....

Questions

1   What is the girl holding?   a ....

2   Where is the dad putting the cake?   on the ....

3   Who is throwing the ball?   the ....

4   Where is the ball now?   on the ....

5   Who has got cake on his face?   ....

Blank Page

Speaking

SCENE PICTURE

Blank Page

OBJECT CARDS

Test 1

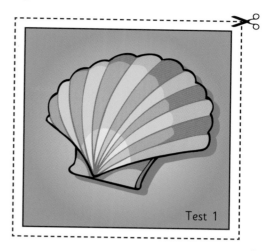

Test 1

Test 1

Test 1

Test 1

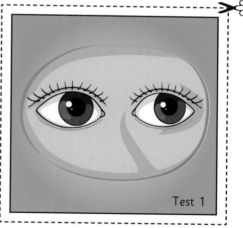

Test 1

Test 1

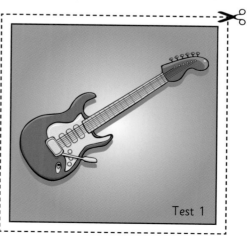

Test 1

Blank Page

SCENE PICTURE

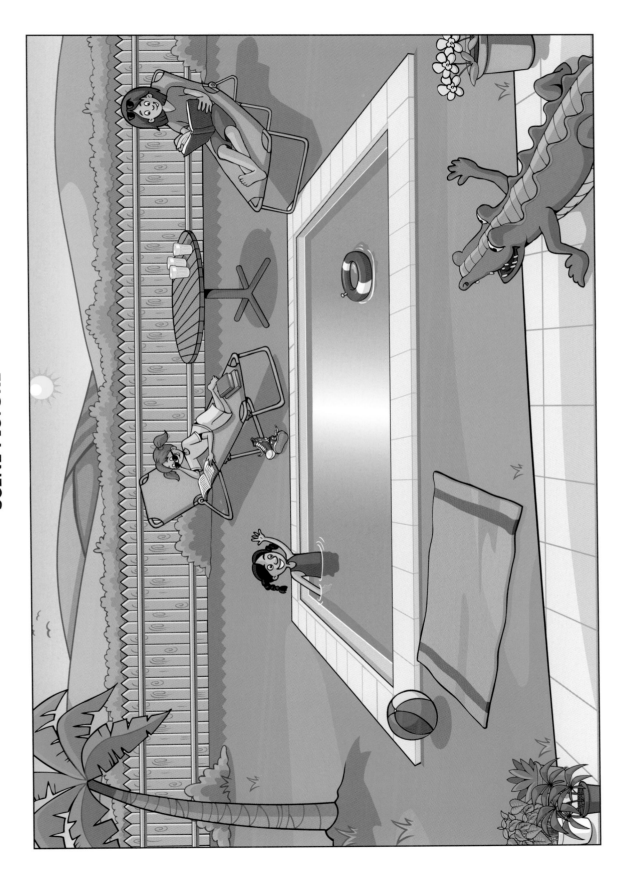

Blank Page

OBJECT CARDS

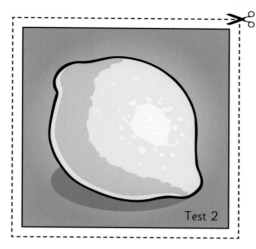

Test 2

Test 2

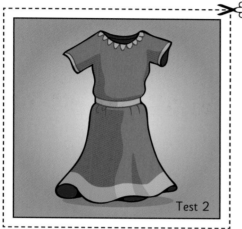

Test 2

Test 2

Test 2

Test 2

Test 2

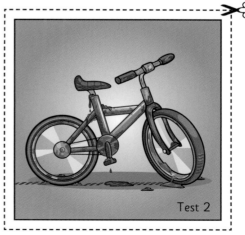

Test 2

Blank Page

SCENE PICTURE

Blank Page